Lacunae

New Poems

Praise for Lacunae

"Once more Scott Cairns's limpid, laconic, beautifully crafted poetry brings us to the brink of language itself, opens us onto the *lacunae*, the gaps the spaces left open to God, waiting to be filled with a mystery beyond words. These guide us, in Cairns's phrase, towards 'many, fleeting, lit lacunae,' each of which 'bids the pilgrim enter' to experience something momentary but also momentous. This is a book to savor slowly and return to often."

—**Malcolm Guite**, author of *Lifting the Veil: Imagination and the Kingdom of God* and other collections

"What I notice first in Scott Cairns' poetry is always his exquisite sense for the beauty of language, a sonic complexity that draws me down the page. Next comes that feeling for a particular mind at work—a mind rich in thought, observation, theology, and wit—a mind always circling unsolvable problems, here figured around the simultaneous elusiveness and presence of the divine, of memory, and of mortality. Always, in *this* book, Cairns considers how the enormous might be contained in the everyday, how the divine can be held in the flash of an image, in a memory, in a thought. I have admired Scott Cairns' brilliant work for many years. He's in top form here."

—**Kevin Prufer**, author of *The Fears*

"These elegantly crafted and spiritually wise poems invite us to change how we see the empty spaces or *lacunae* we typically fill with distractions. Rather, Scott Cairns suggests, what is hollowed may become hallowed, places of encounter with the mystery that calls us to stand outside ourselves—calls us, that is, to ecstasy."

—**Gregory Wolfe**, editor of Slant Books and author of *Beauty Will Save the World* and *Intruding Upon the Timeless*

"If you could remix George Herbert with Wallace Stevens, you might get Scott Cairns. Herbert's theological word play and wit and Stevens' insatiable mind become a kind of continuous prayer in Cairns' newest book, *Lacunae*. For Cairns, language is a form of faith, faith that reaches out towards what is inexhaustible and uncontainable, and faith that trusts words can be a means of coming nearer to what necessarily remains out of reach. Cairns' language roots itself in paradox: words are both 'terminus and new departure'; and fullness draws near only as we become more empty. As in late Stevens, Cairns wants to see 'what is' and, for him, what is inheres in immanence not transcendence, our bodies and the world's body 'abundantly here.' *Lacunae* is the work of a faithful and faith-filled man unafraid of letting his ego be seared, of living in time that continues 'ticking in perplexity.'"

—**Robert Cording**, author of *In the Unwalled City* and other collections

"Scott Cairns is the wisest of poets, a courageous figure who maps the contours and textures of the spiritual life with an exacting eye and ear for the music at the questioning heart of faith. His new book, *Lacunae*, is not only his most ambitious and formally various to date but also the most affecting. 'Every/ word proves every bit as mysterious as/ the Word himself,' he writes, 'and every term proves crux—// both terminus and new departure.' Here is a poet who daily finds in the quotidian inventive means of charting our ever-evolving relationship to the divine. This is a book for the ages."

—**Christopher Merrill**, author of *Flares*

Lacunae

New Poems

Scott Cairns

PARACLETE PRESS
BREWSTER, MASSACHUSETTS

2023 First Printing

Lacunae: New Poems

ISBN 978-1-64060-881-8

The Iron Pen name and logo are trademarks of Paraclete Press.

Library of Congress Cataloging-in-Publication data:
Names: Cairns, Scott, author.
Title: Lacunae : new poems / Scott Cairns.
Description: Brewster, Massachusetts : Iron Pen/Paraclete Press, [2023] | Summary: "Poems that endeavor to contain the uncontainable: just as the Theotokos whose womb contained the uncontainable."-- Provided by publisher.
Identifiers: LCCN 2023021928 (print) | LCCN 2023021929 (ebook) | ISBN 9781640608818 (trade paperback) | ISBN 9781640608832 (pdf) | ISBN 9781640608825 (epub)
Subjects: BISAC: POETRY / Subjects & Themes / Inspirational & Religious | POETRY / American / General | LCGFT: Poetry.
Classification: LCC PS3553.A3943 L33 2023 (print) | LCC PS3553.A3943 (ebook) | DDC 811/.54--dc23/eng/20230512
LC record available at https://lccn.loc.gov/2023021928
LC ebook record available at https://lccn.loc.gov/2023021929

10 9 8 7 6 5 4 3 2 1

Published by Paraclete Press
Brewster, Massachusetts
www.paracletepress.com

Printed in the United States of America

For Marcia, our children,
and grandchildren, etc.

Contents

Recuperating *Lacunae* 17

I. Theoria

Ain't No Meta. Ain't No Nevamind. 21
Time's Favor, etc. 23
Appearances 25
Good Will, Good Fortune 27
Salish Sea Winter 29
Snoqualmie Still Life 31
Old Man's Vision 32
Approaching That Lacuna 34
Mosaic 35
Lacunae 37
Absent Gods 38
Prospect, In Winter 40
Kénosis [*Κένοση*] 41
The End of Suffering 44

II. My Comedy

Aporía [*Απορία*] 47
Coracle 48
My Comedy: Slow Pilgrim 50

Η Θεολογία: God Talk 55
The Presence 58
Adiáphora [Αδιάφορα], Again 59
Mediocrity 61
Remembering "The Death of Ivan Ilyich" and That Man's Late Recovery 62
An Opening, A Glimpse 64
This Cedar Thicket My Acquittal 65
Endless Expanse Within 66
A Reading of Apparent Things 69
For Martyras, Who Fell Asleep at 42, in 2015 73
Change Your Life 75

III. No Transcendence

No Transcendence 79
Butter 81
Clean Kitchen 83
Corner Café, Full Color 84
A School of Embodied Poetics 85
Erotikos Logos, Again 87
Epistle to the Ostensible Church 89
What to Make of This, What to Make 92
Anecdote of the "Poem" Devolved to Anecdote 94
Minor Treatise: *The Poetic* 97
Poem for My Children and Their Children 100
Implicative Lacunae 101

Late Murmur 102
Télos [*Τέλος*] 104

Acknowledgments 107

He made thy body into a throne, and thy womb
more spacious than the heavens.

—Saint John of Damascus, "All Creation Rejoices"

...What worlds, or what vast regions hold
The immortal mind that hath forsook
Her mansion in this fleshly nook...

—Milton, "Il Penseroso"

To see a World in a Grain of Sand
And a Heaven in a Wild Flower
Hold Infinity in the palm of your hand
And Eternity in an hour

—Blake, "Auguries of Innocence"

No plot so narrow, be but Nature there,
No waste so vacant, but may well employ
Each faculty of sense, and keep the heart
Awake to Love and Beauty!

—Coleridge, "This Lime Tree Bower My Prison"

For Occupation – This –
The spreading wide my narrow Hands
To gather Paradise –

—Dickinson, "I dwell in Possibility..."

There is another world, and it dwells within this one.

—Éluard, etc.

Yet a great ring of pure and endless light
Dazzles the darkness in my heart.

It lights the world to my delight.
Infinity is present in each part.

—Madeleine L'Engle

And I now glimpse the miracle by which
the uncontainable was onetime held
within thy woman's womb. And I now glimpse
that Himself bides—ever-present and wholly—
within the least element of creation.

—Isaak the Least

The poetic operation of language—like all
mysteries—occurs with the apprehension
of the inexhaustible within a discrete space.

—Raimundo Luz

And the burning bush? It yet burns, and yet illumines
the pathway of ascent, unconsumed, and ever unconsumed.

—Rabbi Sab

Lacunae

Recuperating *Lacunae*

No, not so much   an emptiness, never yet
an emptiness.   Think, rather, a discrete

cove proving still   to offer—and ever
to offer—what one   cannot, can never,

comprehend, very   like the cup held now
before you, abysmally   full, a pool

roiling with boundless   abundance, this cup
exceeding ken beyond   measure. Endless

abundance, and meet locus   for the sublime,
inexhaustible vastness   for which I

ever ache, yet   observe as primal urge,
unconstrained   by the illusion of space,

our sole occasion   unconsumed by time.

I,
Theoria

Ain't No Meta. Ain't No Nevamind.

Such hard going to step outside
immediate matter, to nudge
the act of interlocution

sufficiently past the sturdy
pale as to accommodate now
anything close to being *έξο*.

Try as one might, one is unlikely
ever to meet with actual
success. Still, even failure proves

informative, as so many
loads of matter—matter *in spades*,
whole shovelsful—are glibly pitched

into the yawning enormity
that spans the heart's adamant hole.
Holy, holy, holy—wholly

implicative of something gone
awry, of something lacking *here*
within the...what? The heart? The soul?

One's noetic architecture
lately fallen in upon itself?
Lord, your alleged mercy would be

sore appreciated should you deign
to have another go at mending
such wretchedness as what we've made

of things. Thank God you seem lately
to have repented of your famous,
ancient wrath, but, then again, your

late reticence appears—from where
we stand blinking—a little too
complete, far too neat. From where we stand

blinking as we gaze up into
a frozen sky, we cannot comprehend
your comprehensive quiet, nor

the countless sparkling lights all
but laughing amid that bleak, broad
immensity above, beyond

which we cannot fathom much.

Time's Favor, etc.

—regarding Χρόνος

What, exactly, *does* time
favor as it chirps along,
a dimly feathered flying
thing undaunted by the blood
and dust collecting on its wings?
Clearly, none of us.

Clearly, none of us much figures
in whatever calculus
performs within the blithe
arc that passes among certain
not-so-discerning congregations
as Providence.

Providence may actually *be*
a thing, but proves nothing
I can wrap my thought around
in terms of time.
That is to say, the God does not
appear to manifest a *timely* care,

no timely care concurrent
with any given, pressing need.
I'm not indicting Him, just
saying that His patent mystery
remains apparently unattached
to what we glimpse as *time.*

The phenomenon of *time*
continues ticking in perplexity,
as I, a fool, keep blinking, hopeful
that love obtains despite
unpromising appearances, for so
I have been told.

Appearances

When what the heart most
craves, most covets, yet appears
as but a glimmer of our
famous, undisclosed
and self-withholding Agent,
full-ensconced behind
each opaque appearance, then
each moot scene is felt
to be a puzzle, and largely
disappointing.

You there—your thumbs fixed
in wonted opposition—
you may as well relax a bit,
or maybe get
a grip. Maybe it's enough
to observe how all
available appearances
appear to glare,
poised, availing a passing
sense of *raison d'être*?

At least—perhaps at best—one
might extend one brave,

solicitous hand to whatever
                    hand yet bides
behind the thinning, the sorely
                    tattered curtain.

Good Will, Good Fortune

Once you quit the gravel road, stepping first
onto the game trail parsing the salal,
you have agreed already to welcome
what is so rarely approached, if in some
deep sense familiar. The damp earth beneath
your boots is oddly welcoming, and the damp
leaves against your thighs a sweet, slow kiss.
And the keen scents of earth, of animal,
and conifer join your breath, softening
your sensible departure from the road.

If you're lucky, you may see just how much
the woodpecker clinging to the hemlock
trunk proves so very like the hemlock trunk;
If you're lucky, you'll observe how even
the hemlock, as well as the cedar, fir,
alder, the sword fern, bracken, and scattered
huckleberry all bear such numinous

life as now the adamant woodpecker
clinging to each subtle undulation
of the hemlock trunk. Yes, all this, with luck.

Salish Sea Winter

Rain all day, and days
    of rain approaching,
the afternoon's gloom
    presses very near—
clouds misting again
    my damp woolen cap,
with the familiar
    confusion of cloud
and woodsmoke failing
    quite to mitigate
my fear of leaving
    undone my morning's work.

My essay presses
    blindly, yet without
much sense of purpose,
    purpose which might have
infused these gray days
    with some slim promise
of light, if dimly
    recollected. Not

quite so likely,
I'm thinking, to hope
that this day will move
much beyond a long-
accustomed chagrin.
Chagrin, and bear it,
yes? Or now succumb
to this dull chill, this
pressure of the air. Still,
if experience
proves yet instructive,
the rain will abate,
and of an evening
the sun may offer
a rose-golden kiss
at its departure,
and if my assay
fails to deliver
simply what I sought,
well, all the better.

Snoqualmie Still Life

Our early snows have closed the mountain pass
in a pristine ermine blanket, and our winds,
unhurried, ripple ever so lightly
the ermine fur.

Our empty road glistens, lined by green conifers
gone white with a late, thick drape of new snow.
Our sky shines blue.

Utterly still, save for the intermittent twitch
of its golden tail, the golden puma
for the moment sits upright, centering
our empty road.

Old Man's Vision

...your old men will dream dreams,
your young men will see visions.

Imagine my surprise, as all along
I had been expecting by this point naught
but dreams, dreams like languid cinematic
recurrences—past fears, past joys, my lost
parents, *et cetera*—each keen absence
rolling without sound, vexingly *sans* speech.

Which is to say that I was ill-prepared
for visions, though I'd seen a good number
in my youth—God's hand, the mother's hand, my own
abrupt demise, quick flash ending the world,
et cetera. In any case, this late
vision began as very like a dream.

My first dog, and my second, then in one
yelping frolic (yes, an audible vision)
all my beloved dogs, my beloved
parents, and grandparents, those I had known
and those I had not, departed friends, all
of us in one broad span, all of us

grinning, laughing, greeting one another
as never before, and that broad expanse
proved so unlike any seen within the bleak
and disappointing dreams with which old men
are all too familiar. The air held light—
so very like the color of beeswax—

and that light held the scent of beeswax, rich
and warm and welcoming as the amber
relics of the saints will warm the pilgrim's
lips, and welcome him, and will fill his lungs
with fragrance and deep calm. This late vision, then,
restored to me some measure of my youth,

when, as I boy familiar with visions,
I stood upon the narrow threshold one
crisp and clear winter night, and raised my eyes.

Approaching That Lacuna

Patmos proves an enigmatic opening. Saint John's cave
affords what might be apprehended

as a close, noetic covert where the pilgrim may yet
find his knees, and, thereafter,

sinking to his knees, might settle deeply into that
most uncommon prayer, which

avails for the riven pilgrim a late return—the mind's
reuniting with the heart. Even

from this far outpost in the West, one might yet appreciate
that much desired recovery of human

aptitude, even here amid the scatter and distraction
that so often dims our poor constituents.

Mosaic

—Ravenna

Drawn from scattered fragments, lifted
by the hand,

this new construction yet obtains
for us a purpose,

a wholeness long desired, long held
and deep beneath these

broken surfaces that have long
comprised

our dissolute appearances,
our grief—still,

each brokenness just now suggests
new purpose,

as each keen edge avails for us
a place to meet

as necessary members, yes,
    and partakers of the all.

Lacunae

The spreading wide my narrow Hands
To gather Paradise—

Say the gift of difficult syntax consists
in the many, fleeting, lit lacunae
glimpsed along the way, obliging the reader's
own intermittent, meandrous detour
along the steep and cobbled path to the dense
sentence's *provisional*—which is to say,
patently *inconclusive—conclusion*.

Say each departure from the path is but
momentary, if each proves also to be,
momentous in its ability to free
both text and reader from too narrow
a grip on the matter at hand, too slight
a distillation of the vertiginous
draught. Each offers humility, and grit.

Duly lit, each glimpsed lacuna bids
the pilgrim enter, invites the pilgrim's
pause amid the silent, open span,
to wonder, and there collaborate,
compels the pilgrim's opening as well.

Absent Gods

These days, few among us fear—nor so much
as consider—the gods. Poseidon, Zeus,

Hades, Hera, all their spoiled, petulant relations—
such figures seldom trouble the late dreams

of the living, distracted as all the living
are obliged to be in their confused slog

across such chafing days as these. Nor, I gather,
do gods as these give any thought to us.

Languishing amid their cool, ambrosial
abundance, they imbibe, quibble, and doze

in uniform dispassion, endlessly
observing the turn of each rough sphere round

its pivot of heat and light. That said, some
among us yet wake anxious in the dark,

quietly made aware of some still, near,
        acknowledging presence pressing its weight—

from within? from without? no telling—pressing
        against our blithe, our dim apprehensions.

Prospect, In Winter

I'm thinking this may prove too little, and far
too late, but I'm hoping yet to shape a brief—
let's say a largely *observational*—sequence,
engaging, and I daresay, questioning
the appearances spread in confusion just
here before me of a gray December day.

As expected, the Salish Sea roughly tosses
its wizened locks in the near distance, one
solid craft appears, braving the choppy bay,
and there beyond the green peninsula
the western ridges rise barely visible above
our ubiquitous band of cloud.

Kénosis [*Κένοση*]

—έαυτον εκένωσεν

Even now, as prelude *to*
—as preparation
for—what is yet to come,
the pilgrim must descend
beneath the din and clatter
of the mind, beneath
the heart's, even the *heart's*,
manifold distractions
unto that stillness dwelling
solely in the *nous*.

It's a little dark, and yes,
not just a little
bleak. Within that dim arena
one also meets
a measure of despair.
Here, this ache, familiar,
attains a strange and
a curious agency,
as if the ache itself becomes
the tool by which
that hollow might obtain
a nascent hallowing.
Many years ago, I chanced
upon the ruins

of Phílippi, accompanied
by George Kaltsás
who led me to that void
of marbled rubble. We
spoke quietly, or not at all
as we wended,
as we wound amid
discrete lacunae, amid
debris, the fallen
artifacts of erstwhile lives.
The effect was efficacious
producing in the gut
an answering emptiness,
and surprising calm.

George was two years past
what had been a terminal
diagnosis, a fate to which
he had responded
with a swim of more
than twenty miles—Kavala
Beach to Thasos, which
he found to be profoundly
emptying of mind,
of heart, of every ounce
of energy. Thus emptied,
he lay still upon
the Thasos shore for days
as his dire emptying

continued, and he sank
beneath all consciousness,
himself. Today, he walks
with me within the ancient
ruins, and so today
he shares with me a glimpse
of what a dread despair
can serve, facilitate
for one whose solitude
opens to an answering
solitude. The God,
he says, remains quite hidden,
but he has had a taste
of how his own erasure
came to offer...what?
Comfort? Consolation? No,
it proved more than that,
more a deep tremor of sudden
expectation, the trembling
thrill of a fullness
drawing near, meeting
one's own becoming emptiness.

—for George Kaltsás

The End of Suffering

The severest pain will send you
to your bed, drop you to the floor.

The severest pain will roll you
into a fetal ball, and squeeze.

Within that grip, you might descend
into your long-abandoned core,

where, mid uncommon darkness, you
may find the door, whose opening

avails at last that lacuna
wherein the *νους** proves yet to be

also more spacious than heaven,
bearing also the Very God,

who is most pleased to meet you there.

*[*νους—nous, often translated as "mind," but better understood as "the intellective aptitude of the heart"]*

II.
My Comedy

Aporía [*Απορία*]

All dressed up, and still
    no place to go. The road
lies choked with unforeseen
    debris. I have misplaced
my keys, and, regardless,
    I don't see any good
reason to start the car.

I have pored above
    this passage for a week.
The prose of Palamás
    proves far too thick a soup
to dish without great care
    even if no amount
of care appears to matter much.

The paradox persists
    beyond my ken—which proves
not a single thing, save
    this: our dear Palamás
knew not to float above
    the text at hand, but knew
one's hope lay ever in descent.

Coracle

When the God inclined to coat himself in clay,
        this many-colored coat of clay we wear,

the clay itself became the holy craft
        by which we venture farther into his

most holy personhood and very light
        comprised of holy personhood he deigned

to share. Take heart. If his inclination
        appears just now to have become a waste

of good intentions, we might just yet effect
        a likely course correction, steering north,

or east—in any case, some yet untried
        direction yielding now a somewhat more

effectual result.
                As most are drawn

to *beauty*, as all desire *joy*, we might
remember each of these is laden with

a measure of descent, that each of these
is sore comprised of suffering. Every

word proves every bit mysterious as
the Word himself, and every term proves crux—

both terminus and new departure. Yea,
our comings and our goings yet appear

to occupy a scene of duly tendered
travel. Your coracle awaits. Embark.

My Comedy: Slow Pilgrim

—all manner of thing will be well

Άδης [Hádes]

Ah, the gates to hell? Just here
behind my eyes. And yes, the gates
remain full open, even as night

descends and I close my eyes, which
serves only to begin a fresh
descent. Have a look. Hell turns out

to be a region of the gut.
Καρδιά? Νους? Whatever. Close enough.
The region of that intellective

ache I surely had suspected
long before this drop into the Dis.
Every wretched denizen

turns out to be my own creation,
and while each is singularly
wretched, my array of grim

malefactors shares a common
complaint—that each was somehow
justifiable, that none was

ever free to be otherwise.
I want to believe them, but I
am not alone, and—given that

I am not alone—I know far
better than to take their word
for anything, especially

for anything so self-serving as
excuse. No one stands alone. Truth
stands ever here among us; Truth

Himself remains just here, attentive
and immovable within my *νους*.
And He will surely not agree

to acquiesce to my poor fictions.

Καθαρτήριο [Cathartírio]

And thus begins, as well, the long
recuperative endeavor,
this harrowing of hell, this late

repair of my disparate
constituents, late cure of my
long belovéd illness. Do I

want to be healed? Let's say I do,
at least today. For the moment,
then, I choose to face Himself,

and in that moment the chagrin
is frankly searing, so I turn
away—though if you *must* know,

one cannot quite turn away, not
any longer. He proves manifestly
present, everywhere. Every angle

proves face-to-face, and so the sear
continues, intermittently
acute, intermittently a bit

diminished, but always keen
to cauterize my wound, my several
cherished wounds. And always, with the sear,

the acrid scent, the smoke, the odd
sense of relief—that finally
I am maybe getting somewhere.

Παράδεισος [Parádisos]

Somewhere turns out to be precisely
where I have always stood, or sat,
or languished unawares. The difference,

now, is that my eyes are open.
And shame or fear or nagging
culpability has been eclipsed

by...what? Willingness? Concurrence?
I would call it a late-recovered
sympathy with *what is*, a desire

to see *what is*, and to apprehend
its comeliness. It appears, here,
at the center of all things—here,

at the center of myself—as
a font, a flower, a blossoming
excess, which I am finally
awake enough to now receive.

Η Θεολογία: God Talk

—Isaak's Epistle

1.

Isaak, late curmudgeon of our Lord
writing to the divers and earnest
lunkheads languishing out yonder,
those several insisting—of so many
astonishing tribes yet and variously
peopling the earth's full, unknowable
expanse—that *Their God*
is not our God. Lord have mercy.

2.

Preposterous brethren, hold your horses.
To the poor extent that any of you can know
anything—to the vexed extent that any
dare speak at all of such profoundly
inscrutable matters—one must know
and must needs aver there is no God but One,

3.

if variously misunderstood, if variously
slighted, if slighted, every time
and unavoidably, by whatever
meager terms of attribution
the yammerers apply in the course

of their incessant yammering. Be still
a moment, and pray without so much
as a single word.

4.
Try it. Try it now.

5.
Forsake your spurious terms, your terminal
illness, your profoundly pinching limits.

6.
The One God is, after all, The Great
*In*terminable, sans conclusion, extending
endlessly far beyond our most expansive
naming, and ever the One surpassing
our every insufficient thought, our every
fraught consideration. Selah.

7.
Anxious in your shuttered enclaves,
chewing your familiar cud, some
among you have on occasion dared point
to the most pious adherents of one
or another alien faith, stammering
their God says such and such; our God says
this here something else

8.

Get a grip. Know this: One God only,
and that God wholly incomprehensible.

9.

Know this: You only know what you can know,
which isn't near enough.

10.

No one hereabouts speaks for God. No one
speaks for God, save God. Sit tight.
You'll know something further of this God,
and very, very soon, and even that, provisional,
and even that insufficient, scant, awaiting
further revelation, further word.

The Presence

As from a dream of wandering, more nearly as from a
dream
of standing lost along a languid river, I woke to find
wafting at the door to my rooms a pale pillar, as of cloud.

Of course, I closed my eyes. I rubbed them, then opened
once again,
during which time the pale cloud had drifted near my bed,
nearly
to my pillow, and stood wavering there, as if awaiting

my consent to its having come so near, its having made
known
to me its presence, which I gathered to have been long-
standing.

As from a dream of coming home, as a dream of arrival
I woke to find the fire standing as a column pressing near.

I knew its heat, was blinded by its light. I rose to meet it
at the door, and at the door I found again the river shore.

Adiáphora [Αδιάφορα], Again

At the kind behest of the belovéd
Father Iakovos, I have another go—
puzzling once again this *adiáphora*.

One more time I quiz its odd constituents
alert as I can manage to what each holds
for those of us yet uncompelled by Stoics,

nor scholastic habits of dismissing what
will not accede to overall consensus.

At the dear behest of Father Iakovos,
I squint to apprehend new matter, substantive,
gleaming with due significance, but free—

untouched by contingency, yet untouched
by complicity and its confining
chains of subsequent, dubious effect.

As analogies go, *sublimity*
    may prove our sole contender—not that it
contends from where it bides beyond our ken.

Just there, beyond appearances, beyond
    the limen of our muddled apprehension,
Sublimity obtains due circumstance.

Indifferent? Sure. Unacknowledged? Well,
    of course. Nonetheless it *is*, causing naught.

Mediocrity

No doubt, our making
    the most of meager
        circumstance can pass
    for something nearly
virtuous. No doubt,
    our gentle applause
        despite the muddled
    school performance serves
as fair evidence
    of our good will. Still,
        one might wince at how
    often one's obliged
to honor the thin
    chagrin of so much
        being made once more
    of yet so little.

Remembering "The Death of Ivan Ilyich" and That Man's Late Recovery

I, too, have meant to say *forgive,*
could only say

forgo, and so, have strayed both *to*
and *fro,* so far

afield from, lo, whatever well-
intended word

I might then have breathed into that
ever lucent

air held just here between us. Words
arriving—as

it were—unsought, unthought, if yet
palpable on

the tongue, humming in the ear, each
time effecting

a further glimpse of all that shines
   far beyond my

own dim wits. I have felt the odd,
   dull ache that brought

to mind the frank, insufficient
   comfort of all

we say we know. I, too, have brought
   two fingers near

my throat to test the pulse trembling
   just there. I would

yet say *forgive*, would yet *forgo*.

An Opening, A Glimpse

Just beyond the pale, the eye
observes a deep lit
shore, and suspects beyond the shore
the sea extending
far as one might yet imagine.

A lesson, then: the pale is failing
to contain the keen
imagination; the pale falls
revealing again
the enormity promising
ever to invite
the soul's complicity in *now*
and ever. I crossed
into that welcoming embrace.

And you? You come, too.

This Cedar Thicket My Acquittal

...Pale beneath the blaze
Hung the transparent foliage...
—Coleridge

This covert offers calm, a brief reprieve
        from the nattering distractions with which
the troubled air is full. Yes, the thicket
        also offers respite from the mind's glib
chatter. One's brief interment mid the leaves
        affords some apprehension of a grave
stillness availing within the heart's warm
        core. Every hidden harbor promises
to every drifting coracle a chance
        to enter and to rest, that attending
to the deeper current's subtle draw, one
        might find the late, noetic cove opening
to all who would ship their oars, and enter.

Endless Expanse Within

—Πλατυτέρα των Ουρανών

Fixed on the sand grains
bright between its toes,
Miss Bishop's sandpiper
continues, keen
to what such grains might yield.
The world is mist,
admittedly vast—what's most
compelling
is how that world remains
at once minute
and vast and clear, like this
grain here, whose light
recalls, of course,
the uncommon vision
beheld by Mister Blake,
his innocent
observation honoring
one's sudden
sense of how immensity
can obtain

within the neat, discrete

occasion of

a grain, an open blossom,

whatever

the hell lies cupped within

your hand, all that

endlessness couched within

your hour—such chance

particulars as these

yet sufficient

to embrace enormity.

The icon

frescoed on the altar's vault

still avers

that the mother whose arms

offer ever-

welcoming embrace

was herself able

to hold, contain

within the pulsing cup

of her womb what

no heaven could contain.

More spacious

than the heavens, we now say,

and in so saying, invoke

a glimpse, brief

taste of what we yet

hold within ourselves.

Knit by knit, within

the pulse, The Very

God's most human body

came to be, came

to bear our dire

occasion, bearing still

the One who cannot be

contained—His all.

A Reading of Apparent Things

As all things are sure to be
        of a sort, as every sort of thing obtains
its own, distinct, reflective opacity,
        one might entertain all such things
as pools, or, say, as open text inviting
        each slow-blinking reader
to lift the book and read.

        Thereafter, duly perused, each
mute thing avails a mostly likely scene
        to which each drowsing reader slowly
wakes to find another day's
        dim consideration, over which,
in short order, the lately wakened reader pores
        with increasingly rapt attention,
and—here, *ephebe*, the late matter's core
        is glimpsed—into which she pours
herself to shape concurrently
        what sort of thing *she* is, and what
said thing involves.

Yes, no doubt, for all appearances
an object has been lately lifted
to the eye, but *no*, no such object
will ever be addressed, *as such*.
The subject must now—must
ever—exert discreet hegemony
upon the thing at hand.

What? You're just now thinking
that you might so simply taste and see?
Hardly. You were supposing
that such discreetly
hidden matter might announce,
unaltered, the unapparent facts
of its essential being? Dream on.
The coffee in your cup is surely
of a sort, as is the cup, as is the needy tongue,
and each performs its meet
collaboration to attain for your
brief moment your momentary sense
of what it is you take into yourself
this blurred and misty morning—
this morning, this morning *only*, as it happens.
The earth—as is *its* habit—has lately

spun just enough to let the sunlight join us
here along the Salish Sea again.

I observed, some small distance from the shore,
a grip of harbor porpoises blithely
rolling south, and saw in nearer water just
beyond the rough and pebbled beach
a single harbor seal floating upright
in the bay and—as it seemed—
meeting my eyes with its own
bright-lit obsidian eyes inflected
by our sun's new amber from the east.
Invisibly, two ospreys sang *kyrie*
from the stand of cedars at my back.
What to make of such a generous array?

I'm making this: whatever waters
one might stand before,
whatever road, whatever thought sees fit
to then accompany whatever scene,
I now suppose one stands along a river—
a common flowing element
that is both uncontained and uncontainable.
I have observed before—somewhere

or other—that one swims ever, necessarily,
  in an abyss, but must insist
that this abyss is not to be mistaken
  for a void, but proves a fullness
unlikely ever to be reduced
  to paraphrase. *Taste and see*, they say.
Read as closely as you can manage.
  The sole, sweet consolation for your patent
incapacity may lie in your now
  knowing that whatever *is* exceeds you.
Selah. Yea. May it be blessed.

For Martyras, Who Fell Asleep at 42, in 2015

—after Cavafy and for Brett Foster

O Isaak, your soul asks that you belatedly
attempt some lines in elegy for our sweet friend
Martyras: some few words, both tasteful and toward.

Maybe you can manage it now, some five years since
his drifting to Abraham's bosom, where—we yet
suppose—he awaits the recovery of all

that he has lost, as well as all that we have lost.
Yes, no doubt that you will speak about his poems, his
wry wrestling with elegant phrasing, his pleasure

in the pun—but say something too of the beauty
of his grin, his easy laughter, his uncommon
gift for friendship extended to those several

of us thus blessed. Isaak, your own phrases often
prove elegant and musical, but we require
an uncommon earnestness just now, entirely

free of irony, free of self-concern. Pour your
unabashed Christian sorrow and Orthodox faith
into these few lines. Isaak, for once, your verses

should disclose the true measure of your grief. Only
in this way will others know that a belated
Alexandrian mourns an Alexandrian.

Change Your Life

—after Rilke's "Archaic Torso of Apollo"

Why must I weep each time
I read again the poem,
that opens me? or when
once more I gaze upon
the great painting, great play?

Why such reflex sorrow
in sore and sharp response
to what I recognize
as the luminous face
of truth's brilliant beauty?

The elusive answer
obtains, as well, in why
an impoverished mind
recoils at each meeting
with corrective wisdom.

The god's broken torso
—yet radiant with wounds—
gleams among those beauties
whose pulse insists that I
be judged, just as I judge.

III.
No Transcendence

No Transcendence

Immanence proves an altogether far
more fitting goal. This trope we figure as
transcendence cannot help but implicate

a false and downright Gnostic severance,
a severe denial of *how* with some
watchful diligence the stuff—the airy

stuff—of spirit may once again be held,
be tendered and absorbed by the body's
salts and oils, the body's sweet confection,

that your whole person may yet comprehend,
comprise a most delicious animal.
I think that it was Coleridge, somewhere

or other, yammering about the sad
habit of first parsing complexity
into its parts, and thereafter dimly

forgetting that the part does not exist
without the whole—a sleight of hand that slights
the abundant and abundantly here.

Butter

—for Stelios Zarganes of Salonika

Unguent of the morning toast, and brightly
effervescent bath for the feathery
morning egg, just so. The sweet *voútiro*
of Greece makes all things more acute, if more
suggestive of the bawling goat, its scent.

In Italy, the *burro* breaks one's heart
with mild, mute solicitude there mingling
the *umbricelli* with the fragrant pea.
Trekking once through the furnace of the vast,
green Halkidikí, I chanced upon

three goatherds at their midday meal, and fell
readily into my chosen role as famished
Xéno, foolish *Xéno* unprepared. Their coarse
rusks proved most elegant pallets
for the curds, the *thrombas*, the bit of fish.

At their grill, mid the *tsípouro* and cool *krasí*,

they toasted slabs of wheat bread, which we smeared

with *voútiro* and thyme. Much later, as I packed

to leave the belovéd city, the belovéd Stélios

gave to me a jar of butter. Think of it: a jar of butter.

Clean Kitchen

Upon its pristine surfaces I lay
        the day's provisions—sea bream glistening

on white tile, the shallot and the leek, one
        bright red carrot, accompanied by one

vivid yellow, one stalk of the modest
        celery. I have yet to raise my knife,

but look, before us, already a feast.

Corner Café, Full Color

Of course, the foie gras is nicely done, the pink
        of a dusty rose, perfectly formed, with green

onion, red peppercorn, a grating of black
        truffle pretty much upping the ante, luminous,

as all of the above lies set in a deep red
        and glistening jus. Just so. You're hungry, yes?

A School of Embodied Poetics

—for Jeffrey Pethybridge

Sure enough, bodies fail, but their failure
proves relatively brief; their failure proves
not to be forever. What proves to be

everlasting is the final wedding
of spirit and flesh. Meantime, each parting
most of us will suffer turns out to be

but trial separation, not to be
mistaken for anything like a sad
conclusion. Biting into what turned out

to be a very ripe peach, the juices
glistening my whiskered chin, I chanced
upon this passing thought. All poetics,

per se, must have to do with making, must
have to do with stuff—the glistening matter
at hand, say, as well as the bodily

response to whatever it is the shaper
shapes. My wife happened into the room, just
as I was imagining another

airy stanza. *Enough*, I thought, *enough*.

Erotikos Logos, Again

There is a most vain class among men,
those despising ordinary things,
fixing their eyes upon distances,
pursuing empty air with faint hopes...
—Pindar

As a boy, I met a good many of these, praying
in church. In most churches,

even now, one can witness the *ethereal*
sneaking in to rob the body of its substance.

An unfortunate taste for transcendence
manages yet to erode the mountain

of its immanence, allowing for a thin
and unsatisfying dream of unencumbered

spirit to hold an airy hegemony. Such severe
and severing demands of the sacred

render it bodiless, biding ever elsewhere, if at all.

Such persons prefer dream to flesh, prefer that
    even their Holy One

remain both untouchable and unlikely to touch.

Epistle to the Ostensible Church

Your fond Isaak, latecomer to the slog,
sometime schmoozer among the blathering
heretics, if lately a little bit
judge-y, a little peeved concerning the blithe,
ubiquitous, and widespread ignorance
tolerated among slacker Xians,
whose glib disdain for their own history,
whose disinterest in pursuing much
if any progress along that ancient
path leaves me blinking, open mouthed—and, yes,
increasingly cranky—as each week brings
yet another earnest attempt to re-
invent the wheel, or to send it rolling
to the ditch. Peace.
                                        I write to all y'all
hunkered within your separate enclaves
to puzzle out why your neatly pared down
faith so seldom satisfies the vacuum
of your God-obsessive appetites. Peace.

That we are all adopted—appallingly
co-opted into Christ's holiness—is
a simple *given*, and a certainty.
So relax. His good pleasure will surely
accommodate at some future end-time
our patent sloth and habitual dim-
wittedness. Meantime, have a stretch.
The faith
you hope to grasp is not so much a grip
of propositions, and most surely not
that queer array of anxious codes with which
you have replaced the parabolic puzzle
that the fathers taught; such reductions keep
the body blind, mostly deaf, forever
not just a little dumb.
Suppose a more
efficacious grip would come of lifting
your hand to take the cup—with fear and faith
and love, to part your lips, receiving what
is borne upon the spoon. The cup is not
so much a good idea as it is
your very life, one portion sunk into
your hungry gut, the animating spirit

joined unto an elemental and a bright
result, joining your sad persons to one
trembling joy investing all and everything
with theanthropic agency.

Remember

to love one another, and please forgive
your cranky Isaak, whose love for you may
yet prove—please, O God—incorruptible.

What to Make of This, What to Make

—Isaak's epistle

Isaak, dim and grinning servant, sometime
scribe, to the scattered, blinking latecomers
just now waking to our long, common slog
through meandering marshlands, deserts, right
chafing storms of circumstance: Yo! Condolences.

The challenge may appear uncommonly
arduous of late, but the challenge has
always been thus: a strenuous matter
demanding we apply every scrap of wit,
hope, our senses of humor, and creative ken—

all of these brought to bear as tools to tweak
the mess extending far as we can see
and—from what we might gather—a good bit
farther. The challenge, yea, the endless chore
remains that we must each make something new of all

that lay before us, all that lay behind.
Imagination, duly understood,

proves yet to be the cupola, our most
revealing due inheritance, owned by
our having been created in His Image. Lo.

So, yes, the challenges ahead lie fraught
with new demands yet mixed with prior sins,
and these have caused a clamor, deafening
the ears of those who might have rectified
the past, who must yet listen more attentively.

The sighs, the tears, the angry cries arising
provoked by generations unconcerned,
denying all conviction—that's the mess
each soul is now obliged to mitigate,
the new construction to which all must lend a hand.

I'm in. In His Image, each is vastly
well-endowed to turn the heart, the mind, all
noetic agency to this endless
task—imagining the road ahead, there-
after setting out to build it as we go. Just so.

Anecdote of the "Poem" Devolved to Anecdote

Most egregious, you might think, most
regrettable—as each now lifeless

term turns too readily into
terminus, or mere sign whose

listless finger can only point
to some *this* or *that* moment poised

drowsing in the past—is the way the not-
quite-poem thereby can no longer

sustain *poiesis* as such, can
no longer serve as ongoing

scene of generation, cannot
so much as entertain the yet-

to-be, our dear future. Suppose,
instead, a jar placed upon a hill;

imagine its lit transparency
as an invitation to see,

as through a clear portal, to see
by the mind's tall, generative power

a little something new, a new-
made something, a vessel holding

more, suggesting more than you had thought
to place therein. As an anecdote merely,

any little boat proves far too likely to sink
beneath recovery, and any gear

you hoped to find on board crumbles
in the hand. As an anecdote merely

the sweetest coracle fills with muck,
and—trust me!—languishes, dead

in the water, nor can it prove
harbor where one's mind—nor any

other mind—might find occasion
to drift a bit, unpack its unsuspected

hold, savor mid those waters the span
of implication where we live.

Minor Treatise: *The Poetic*

proves to be
an operation
of language,
wherein
the presence
and activity
of inexhaustible,
indeterminate
enormity is even so
apprehended
in a discrete space.

Think *Theanthropos.*
Think *Logos tou Theou.*

That's a little heady. Yes,
that's a little
much. Still,
I'll need you
to up the ante

re: what it is

you expect

a poem to do.

If it refers, merely,

if it points away

from itself, overmuch,

to one or another

profound event

or thought preceding

the moment

of the poem,

the imposter fails

to be a poem; it fails

to make, fails

to occasion

anything approaching

generative agency

on the page, and you

have got yourself

a heartbreak

on the way.

Failing in this, it will
   further fail
to enhance
   the previous,
which, after all, is
   precisely what
the *poem* must *do*—
   it must *make*
a new thing, even while
   employing some
prior thing
   generously given,
and received,
   and put to work.

Poem for My Children and Their Children

Sure, not counting a wrong turn—
        or several wrong turns—along the way,
not counting the switchbacks
        —each of which led me
        to thinking how slowly I was
        getting nowhere—
not counting the several slick spots
        among salal, sword fern, and bracken
        that have sent me to my knees
        upon the mud trail, the slope,
not counting the two or three
        occasions when the foaming.
        glacier-floured river proved
        almost too compelling an end,
I would have to say the trek
        has been vigorous
        and very good.

Implicative Lacunae

...It was like
A new knowledge of reality.
—Stevens

Entering the clearing, he knew
that he had heard it, the single
note expanding beyond the reach
of any single note, as if,
finally, his dim ideas
about things showed themselves to be
stick figures failing to evince
the fullness of the body. She
said to him *so, at long last you*
have heard it, yes? He stood just there
at the clearing's edge, daring not
to speak. He closed his eyes that he
might better listen, and the note
became a space like the clearing
into which all that could be sung
found dwelling, and he became
like a man without a doctrine,
became a man intent on praise,
a man whose freedom would ever
expand, would ever reach toward.

Late Murmur

—this familiar pulse beginning
in the throat

Could it be the heart's late attempt to call
attention to itself, a stuttered nudge
that the pilgrim pause just now to attend

to time's deleterious effects? Yes,
it *might could be* exactly that. My heart's
just fine, for now. How's yours? One needn't wait

for calamity to consider course
correction, nor even to entertain
recourse altogether. Evening

proves a likely time for reappraisal.
This evening, I notice, to the west,
how little snowpack remains trenched upon

the western range. The evening haze has
thickened, coloring the mountains a faint
blue, one shade darker than the western sky.

This evening, the familiar pulse sends
its recurrent, if mostly neglected
message: *mercy, mercy, mercy, mercy.*

Télos [*Τέλος*]

Imagine now an end that is itself
unending, a calyx opening
past the tick of time, an end without
conclusion. Yes, that is what I now
suppose as τέλος, the slim stem of time
blossoming, as a fountain whose bright
waters forever flow up, flow out,
in which we live and move, and ever.

Acknowledgments

The following poems initially appeared as follows:

"Ain't No Meta. Ain't No Nevamind." and "Kénosis [Κένοση]," *The Christian Century*

"Mosaic," lyrics accompanying the music CD *Ravenna* by Jeff Johnson and Phil Keaggy

"Approaching That Lacuna," *Ergon: Greek/American Arts and Letters*

"My Comedy: Slow Pilgrim," appearing in *Divining Dante*, edited by Paul Munden and Nessa O'Mahony

"Epistle to the Ostensible Church," *Image: Art, Faith, Mystery*

"What to Make of This, What to Make," *Imagination in an Age of Crisis*, edited by Jason Goroncy and Rod Pattenden

"Aporía [Απορία]," *Ad Fontes*

"This Cedar Thicket My Acquittal" and "No Stranger," *Relief: A Journal of Art and Faith*

"Late Murmur" and "The End of Suffering," *Ekstasis*

"Coracle," *Jacob's Well*

Earlier versions of the following poems also appeared in *A School of Embodied Poetics,* a limited edition chapbook published in 2020 by Paraclete Press: "Erotikos Logos, Again," "Good Will, Good Fortune," "Snoqualmie Still Life," "Approaching That Lacuna," "Absent Gods," "Η Θεολόγια: God Talk," "*Adiáphora [Αδιάφορα]*, Again," "Remembering 'The Death of Ivan Ilyich' and That Man's Late Recovery," "Minor Treatise: *The Poetic,*" "Butter," and "A School of Embodied Poetics."

O that my words were written down!
O that they were inscribed in a book!
O that with an iron pen and with lead
they were engraved on a rock forever!

—Job 19:23–24

Outcast and utterly alone, Job pours out his anguish to his Maker. From the depths of his pain, he reveals a trust in God's goodness that is stronger than his despair, giving humanity some of the most beautiful and poetic verses of all time. Paraclete's Iron Pen imprint is inspired by this spirit of unvarnished honesty and tenacious hope.

OTHER IRON PEN BOOKS

Andalusian Hours, Angela Alaimo O'Donnell

Begin with a Question, Marjorie Maddox

The Consequence of Moonlight, Sofia Starnes

Cornered by the Dark, Harold J. Recinos

Eye of the Beholder, Luci Shaw

Exploring This Terrain, Margaret B. Ingraham

From Shade to Shine, Jill Pelaez Baumgaertner

Glory in the Margins, Nikki Grimes

Idiot Psalms, Scott Cairns

Iona, Kenneth Steven

Litany of Flights, Laura Reece Hogan

Raising the Sparks, Jennifer Wallace

There Is a Future, Amy Bornman

To Shatter Glass, Sister Sharon Hunter, CJ

Wing Over Wing, Julie Cadwallader Staub

About Paraclete Press

Paraclete Press is the publishing arm of the Cape Cod Benedictine community, the Community of Jesus. Presenting a full expression of Christian belief and practice, we reflect the ecumenical charism of the Community and its dedication to sacred music, the fine arts, and the written word.

www.paracletepress.com